This Journal Belongs to:

Name ....

Email ....

Telephone ....

Breathe

Thrive

JOURNAL

STERLING
New York

Thrive

Most people have goals and aims—hopes and dreams of the things they want to get out of life, that perfect job they'd love to do, the once-in-a-lifetime experience they've dreamed of since childhood, or even just making a habit of a simple action that might mean their day-to-day life is a little brighter.

Sometimes though, when life has become a checklist of things you have to do and places you need to be, those wants and desires can feel remote and out of reach. You've lapsed into survival mode, doing just enough to keep going, and everything feels stressful, overwhelming, and unsustainable. If only you had a bit more time or a bit more money, or were a bit less tired, you think to yourself. You could escape the trap and take those dreams off hold.

Changing this mindset is the first step to taking action, and that's where this journal can help. Brought to you by the creators of *Breathe* magazine, the simple exercises and prompts can be used to find ways to put yourself first, work out what you truly want, and move past the barriers that are holding you back. It's time to stop just surviving and start thriving.

Breathe

breathemagazine.com

Contents

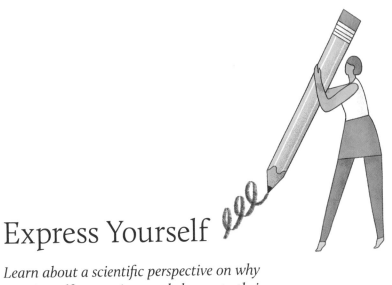

Express Yourself

Learn about a scientific perspective on why creative self-expression can help you to thrive.

Unlike animals, humans evolved to use art and language as a mechanism to express interests and points of view without the need for violence. This powerful tool has led to countless celebrated works that have changed the world: from Shakespeare and Renaissance masterpieces influencing early Western society to successful campaigns driving public behavior, such as those for HIV/AIDs prevention. But to understand its potential, we need to delve into the science behind self-expression.

Ancient Patterns

There's a part of our brain referred to as the reptilian brain, which is common in other animals and responsible for instincts. Every time you feel threatened, this part of the brain releases hormones to alert you of danger and then rewards you if you successfully overcome the risk you were facing. This happens because this ancient part of the brain is obsessed with survival.

When the brain senses it's in a vulnerable situation, it immediately releases the stress hormone cortisol, signaling the importance of getting away from a dangerous situation as quickly as possible. To the brain, cortisol feels as startling as an early alarm during the weekend. And when the person jumps into action, either by confronting or abandoning the vulnerable condition they're facing (fight-or-flight), the alarm stops, and the brain releases feel-good chemicals when you resolve the situation. This release leads to emotions such as joy, calm, trust, and sense of achievement.

Human vs. Animal

In the animal world, when a creature is at risk, it reacts solely through actions—attacking or fleeing. But humans have learned another way to achieve goals or approach uncomfortable situations, and that's by using self-expression. As Loretta Graziano Breuning, author of *The Science of Positivity* and founder of the Inner Mammal Institute in California, says, "People learned to fight without the need to inflict physical harm and to flee without really running away." You can tap into the fight-or-flight mechanism when you express yourself, either verbally or visually, especially in difficult times. In other words, self-expression is a positive and safe way to mitigate the signs of distress sent by your reptilian brain.

Modern-Day Survival

Now let's think conceptually about art and self-expression from the viewpoint of a resting state of mind when you aren't perceiving any risks, in order to understand why humans feel good when they express themselves. When the need to communicate arises—through art and words—the brain releases dopamine. This hormone is emitted in anticipation of you taking steps to satisfy a need. In this case, that need is the desire to make your feelings and opinions tangible. That's why your brain rewards you for even thinking about transmitting and sharing an idea, through visual or verbal language, giving you a feeling of satisfaction. Self-expression is part of a survival instinct rewarded by your brain.

Tough Terrain

Some believe the ideal terrain for self-expression is pain and crisis. This makes a lot of sense when it's understood as a mechanism of defense. Let's see what happens when the reptilian brain works in conjunction with the part that thinks and analyzes—the prefrontal cortex. The eyes and other senses are always scanning to find as many threats as possible, searching for valuable information that confirms situations of vulnerability. That information is transmitted directly to the brain, where the prefrontal cortex makes multiple associations and conjectures, stimulating the release of cortisol and triggering opinions, statements, and actions related to what the individual considers to be the best thing to say or do to "promote survival."

Necessary Release

For this reason, self-expression emerges as a powerful tool for human beings in difficult times—it's a form of catharsis. Portraying and making thoughts and emotions tangible in times of difficulty is natural and necessary. Many health experts believe that what's left unsaid could manifest itself in more harmful ways in people's physical health. For the ancient Greeks, catharsis meant purifying the soul by contemplating a situation that was considered tragic.

Nowadays, with so many tools and communication channels at everyone's fingertips, the definition of catharsis has moved on from solely contemplating emotions and instead alludes to an overproduction of self-expression—which is perfectly fine. From a scientific perspective, self-expression is a healthy way to respond to the stimuli around you, regardless of whether there's a real crisis or if you simply need to express yourself and enjoy the good feeling caused by the flow of dopamine.

USING ART FOR CATHARSIS

Here are two ways to make difficult emotions tangible:

1. Paint It Out
Use colors that best represent your mood. Grab a big canvas and let your thoughts out through abstract lines and shapes.

2. Build It in Clay
Get some air-dry clay and give your emotions a form. Doing something so tactile adds an extra enjoyable element.

The Role of Writing

Writing can be thought of as an act of magic—when you write, your conscious and structured thoughts or unconscious and unnoticed feelings become visible letter by letter, word by word. In fractions of seconds, your fingers create what your brain is telling them to—it's amazing. And when those thoughts, abstractions, interpretations, and associations are brought together and made visible, they can be read as if they weren't yours. They can be understood from a totally new perspective, allowing your brain to reinterpret and resignify what you wrote to give it a deeper meaning or simply distance itself from what has been written. It's like a ping-pong game where the winner is mental health.

Why Is Writing Effective?

Writing stimulates neural connections and releases dopamine, reducing cortisol levels released by the brain when it perceives risk or the imminent need to communicate. Dopamine is also released when you feed your brain new information through reading fresh material. Both reading and writing are therapeutic tools that stimulate your brain in positive ways and are, best of all, at the reach of your fingertips. Any word or idea that arises from your conscious or unconscious brain and positively adds to and generates conversation energizes your mind and soul in healthy ways. At the same time, writing will also inspire any other individuals you collaborate with—perhaps even influencing society.

FINDING FLOW

Any repetitive creative motion that delivers a result will flood your brain with dopamine. Here are a few to try:

- Play a musical instrument.

- Practice a sport, whether it's tennis, mountaineering, or golf.

- Try your hand at knitting.

- Take up photography.

- Learn a new language.

- Complete a crossword.

WRITE IT OUT

Create your own personal acts of magic and enjoy the many benefits that come from self-expression.

1. Dear Me
Free-write a letter to yourself. Read and release what you normally don't say out loud. You don't have to edit yourself. Write down what comes.

2. Tell Your Story

Everyone has a story and yours could be more powerful than you ever thought. Use this space for planning and jotting down notes about key events in your life. Focus on the emotions that are brought up.

....

....

....

....

....

....

....

....

....

....

....

....

....

....

....

....

....

....

To Do or Not To Do?

You're more likely to thrive when you take on what you want to do instead of what you think you ought to do.

Do you often bite off more than you can chew? Does this then usually end up with you feeling exhausted and guilty for not doing all the things you said you would? If so, you're not alone. In a culture that rewards productivity and busyness, it can be tempting to accept everything that's slung your way, regardless of how snowed under or frazzled you may feel. However, this can lead to burnout and underlying feelings of resentment. But what's the alternative? It all comes down to the choices you make, how much you're prepared to take on, and how much you let go.

How Much Can You Chew?

Different people have different capacities for taking on extra tasks, be it work, social engagements, hobbies, family requirements, or community activities. Things as simple as personality, lifestyle, fitness level, and stage of life all have an impact on how much you can handle in day-to-day life. So, how do you know how much to take on? Think about a few normal days (not vacations or special occasions) that you consider as good ones. Then consider the days that you feel were bad. Compare the two in terms of how much activity you did. Perhaps your good days were ones where you bounced from task to task with barely a pause in between, or maybe they included just one activity in the morning and another in the afternoon, with plenty of time to be still or quiet in the middle. Thinking about what your ideal schedule looks helps you take a step toward making sure you are not over- or underburdened.

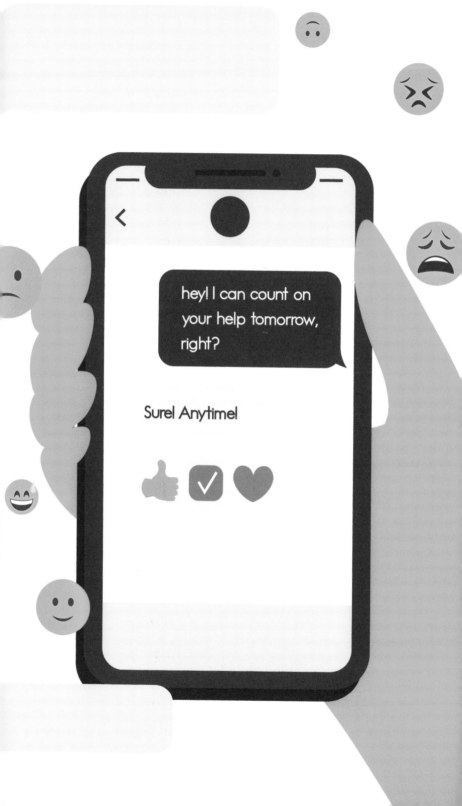

Ephemeral Obligations

Of course, you don't always have a huge amount of say in what you do, as there are many things that simply have to be done—some perhaps through no choice of your own. At different stages in life, there are different priorities, commitments, and capacities. The workload of a college student, for instance, will be different from that of a full-time employee, which will again vary from that of a stay-at-home mom (and so on and so forth). It's helpful to think of life being made up of seasons, which change as time passes. For instance, when taking on a new and demanding job, or in the early years of motherhood, you're likely to have a lot less spare time than you did before. But knowing that it's a season that will soon change into another where you have more time for other things (because you've got used to the job, or your children have started school) can help you not feel as swamped by your current commitments. In times like this, know that you'll need to say "no" to more things than in other seasons.

Positives vs. Negatives

Aside from your usual routines, there are countless other things you might agree to: your brother asks you to babysit, your boss needs you to take on an extra project at work, your best friend wants you to join a dance class with them, you'd like to learn a new language. So, how do you determine which things you should say yes to, and which things no? Activities that get an affirmative answer are often easier to take on—if something sounds like it would bring you joy, say yes. If you really want to help out somebody you care about, say yes. If the work project sounds like a blast, say yes. Sometimes the negatives are straightforward, too. You really hate dancing, for instance, or you know you genuinely don't have the time for something. But what happens when you're not so sure? A classic pros and cons list can be helpful. Write out what the outcomes and repercussions would be from saying yes or no to a certain activity. If the positives outweigh the negatives, go for it! What if it all seems positive, but you really can't cram one more thing into your timetable? Think about what else could go. According to global marketing research firm Nielsen, the average American adult spends more than four hours a day watching TV, and three hours and forty-five minutes interacting with their smartphone. Assess your time with these things and others, and consider how much value they add to your day.

What If You're Conflicted?

Sometimes, of course, saying either yes or no is more complicated than this, with your heart, your head, your planner, and your wallet all pulling you in different directions. There's often a feeling of guilt that accompanies saying yes to something when the heart knows that no is a better response, or vice versa. This can occur when things are done for the sake of other people, rather than for the activity itself. That's not to say that it's wrong to serve others in what you do, but that you shouldn't do things because of what others will think. Do you want to help your brother out because it'll make you look better than your sister, who never helps? Is learning a new language attractive because you want to sound impressive on that business trip? Are you reluctant to start that new hobby because you're worried it's not trendy?

Thinking about the motives for doing or wanting to do something is important and can usually resolve the feeling of conflict. In his book *The Freedom of Self-Forgetfulness*, theologian Timothy Keller says that the key is "not thinking more of myself or thinking less of myself, it is thinking of myself less." He calls this the freedom of self-forgetfulness and goes on to say that by paying less attention to how others view him, "I can start to enjoy things that are not about me. My work is not about me, my skating is not about me, my romance is not about me, my dating is not about me. I can actually enjoy things for what they are."

FORGET YOURSELF

Paying less attention to the way others view you can free you up to enjoy things that help you to thrive.

1. Saying Yes
Think of a time when you said yes to something against your better judgment. How did it make you feel? What were the consequences? How did it impact your schedule, energy levels, and mood?

Write down your thoughts here in a stream of consciousness.

....

....

....

....

....

....

....

....

....

....

....

....

....

....

2. Saying No

Now consider what would have happened if you'd said no. How would you have felt? What would you have done instead? Maybe you would have had more time to spend with a friend after a busy week, perhaps you would have progressed further with a creative project that always brings you a sense of calm—or you might have just done nothing at all, and felt grounded and ready for the next day.

Write down your alternative reality, being as imaginative as you like and paying close attention to your feelings.

....

....

....

....

....

....

....

....

....

....

....

....

....

....

Clear the Fear

It's rational to feel apprehensive about making big decisions, but being too afraid can hold you back from making creative choices that could enhance your everyday life and bring about a more fulfilled future. How do you put fear in its rightful place and stop it from taking charge?

Whether it's opting to move, taking the leap into a new job, or leaving a relationship, making a big change can feel daunting. We can't see into the future to find out what the consequences of our choices will be, and sometimes we let fear of the unknown, or of change itself, cloud our decision-making. But fear doesn't have to drive what we do. If we stop allowing it to determine our decisions, we can take control of our destiny and future.

Ancient Origins

Fear is there for a reason: when our ancestors lived in constant danger of being killed by wild animals, the adrenaline-fueled fight-or-flight response kept them from harm. But this primitive part of our brains still creates feelings in response to things that don't warrant such a reaction. "It's there to keep us safe ultimately, but it has no reckoning of the true measure of 'danger' we're in," says coach and mentor Lynette Allen. "Unless we are running away from true personal danger, fear will try to do its job even when there is no actual danger. Generally, fear doesn't make good decisions, and if you don't recognize fear for what it is, it will take you over and become you."

Life coach Katie Phillips says beliefs formed in childhood can let fear take hold of our lives. But they don't have to run the show. "Our life experiences and childhood conditioning create belief systems that unconsciously guide our day-to-day life and decision-making," she explains. "Often we create stories in our heads about what's true without challenging them, because we are on autopilot and not conscious that those stories are running our lives. Fear-based belief systems are organizing most people's lives because they haven't chosen to get conscious and notice the rules they are living by."

You vs. Fear

Being aware that fear is forcing its way in when we need to make a decision can help us rationalize our thinking. "You are actually two separate things: you . . . and fear," says Lynette. "Fear is not you. When you know that, you can ask yourself, 'Is this fear talking?' or 'Is this love talking?' The opposite of fear is always love, and once you get into the habit of seeing fear as separate from you, you start to see how it influences your decisions. Once we've mastered the difference between us and fear, we can make decisions we choose."

When we allow deep-seated beliefs that come from a place of fear to make our decisions, we're stopping ourselves from reaching our potential. "When unchallenged, fear-based belief systems are running the show, we are not living our fullest, most authentic lives," explains Katie. "We play small and don't allow ourselves to shine. We are not hooked into the truth of who we are and so are not tapped into or honoring our deepest desires. Life feels hard rather than the joyful, happy existence we actually have the choice to experience."

Flip the Script

The fearful state of mind that comes from our limiting beliefs can be changed, allowing us to empower ourselves and our decision-making. "Mantras such as 'I am safe,' breathing techniques, talking it out, hugging it out, and writing it out are all excellent ways, if you are committed, to understand the difference between you and fear," says Lynette.

Katie, meanwhile, advises questioning your own beliefs. "When we challenge conditioned rules we are able to witness how we have been limiting ourselves. When we choose new rules and new beliefs, life becomes unlimited. When we believe we are good enough, that anything is possible, and that we are worthy of our heart's desires, suddenly life becomes an exciting adventure."

Ask the Questions

Questioning what is influencing our decisions is the key to creating the life we want, free from fear. "I love the acronym for fear: False Evidence Appearing Real," says Katie. "Whenever a fearful thought shows up, I ask myself, 'Is that true?' I challenge the fear-based belief. Getting conscious and reprogramming our limiting, fear-based beliefs is a game-changer to creating a peaceful, joyful, abundant life."

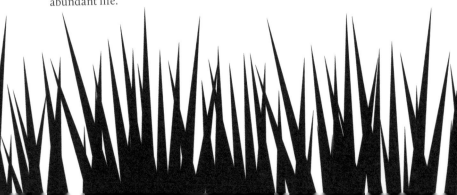

YOUR FEAR-BUSTING TOOL KIT

When you feel reluctant to enact change or make big decisions, remember that it may not be you talking but fear. Use the following prompts to get mindful about who's running the show, then use this awareness to replace your fear with love.

Describe the big decision or change here.

....

....

....

....

Now imagine yourself following through with it, without any barriers, either from yourself or others. What would happen? How would you feel? How would that emotion change? Be as detailed as you like, but the more in-depth, the better, as exploring the subject fully will help you understand your feelings toward it.

....

....

....

....

....

....

....

....

....

....

....

Now imagine the opposite—you didn't go through with the decision. What would happen? How would you feel? Again, be as detailed as you like.

....

....

....

....

....

....

Go to a trusted person in your support network and talk to them about each scenario—if you like, you can show them what you've written. Ask for their honest opinion about what they think you should do. Now consider your reluctant response. Ask yourself, "Is this fear talking?" If you think it's fear, how would your response be different if it came from love?

....

....

....

....

....

....

....

....

....

....

Personify your fear to help separate it from you. Draw a sketch of what your fear looks like. Give it a name and some character traits to make it real.

BREATHE OUT THE FEAR

Next time you find yourself feeling overwhelmed by a worry or fear, try this simple breathing exercise.

- Set a timer for five minutes.

- Sit in a comfortable position, somewhere you won't be disturbed, and close your eyes.

- Slow down your breathing, so you're inhaling for a count of five and exhaling for a count of five.

- With every inhale, say to yourself, "I am brave."

- With every exhale, say to yourself, "I am safe."

- After the time is up, check in with how you feel and sit and reflect for a few moments.

- Now tell your embodiment of fear, "Thank you for your help. I know you're trying to keep me safe, but I've got this—you won't be making this decision."

Close Encounters

Scared of letting people in? Or know someone whose true self, try as you might, you just can't see? It could be issues with intimacy—it's vital for a thriving relationship, and there's more to its avoidance than being shy.

Visualize someone who shies away from intimacy—the image of an outgoing person who's usually surrounded by others is probably not what springs to mind. Surely such people are introverts, avoiding company and preferring to keep themselves tucked up in their own private worlds? Yet it's exactly this kind of assumption that allows those who struggle with or avoid intimacy to remain hidden from others and to ignore or deny their own tendencies. Just as there's a difference between being alone and being lonely, it's also true that there's one separating those who are always among people and those who are intimate with others. Contrary to popular belief, extrovert behavior, success, and seemingly effortless social integration is often at the heart of intimacy evasion.

What Is Intimacy?

Often thought of in terms of romance or sexuality, intimacy is just as relevant to friendships and family relationships. It's to do with letting others really get to know you—and the vulnerability that comes with it. This is why those who fear it are often the life and soul of a gathering—the ability to entertain and engage many people provides the ideal curtain behind which to hide when keeping others at arm's length.

Intimacy is a closeness and familiarity in a relationship that can be open, unguarded, relaxed, and mutually understanding. It's the ability to share and comes, according to experts, in four variations:

- Emotional—expressing significant feelings
- Experiential—an open attitude to experiencing things with another person
- Intellectual—feeling comfortable to express one's opinions, ideas, and thoughts with someone else
- Sexual—genuine physical closeness with another

What Prompts Avoidance?

Fear of loss is generally at the heart of most intimacy-related concerns—whether it's losing emotional breathing space (engulfment) or someone who matters (abandonment). By keeping others at bay, the avoidant person believes that they can protect themselves from these scenarios. Low self-esteem and feelings of unworthiness may cause some to fear evaluation—the idea of others talking about "the real them" is excruciating and, for that reason, they remain largely unknowable, even in social settings. In many cases, some or all of these factors may even coexist and, like many fears, it can be difficult to pin these to one single event or moment in time. They may stem from having experienced neglect or death, or from feeling overwhelmed by the emotional needs of others. Though the seeds for such tendencies are often sown in childhood, they can also be attributed to later-life events that leave a pattern-setting scar. Certain individuals may be able to recognize their own intimacy-avoidant behaviors, as well as the life events that triggered them; however, these are often likely to be unearthed and discussed in a therapeutic environment.

Is Therapy Really Necessary?

While solitude is both healthy but essential to well-being, we also need human connection to thrive, as outlined in psychologist Abraham Maslow's Hierarchy of Needs theory. A lack of social interaction can adversely impact mental and physical health, but, importantly, it isn't necessarily the number of relationships that is an accurate measure of connection. Rather, it's the emotional bond and attachment that's experienced within a relationship that makes the difference. If a person's ability to form such connections is affecting their well-being, then it might be beneficial to seek professional advice.

What Are the Signs?

Some of the patterns typically displayed by an avoidant person can be difficult to read because they convey mixed signals. Much of their behavior can easily be taken as social competence and fullness of life, making it easier for avoiders to hide behind and suppress the reasons for these behaviors from themselves.

Busyness is one example—someone who's always in the middle of hundreds of projects, arrangements, and engagements will probably look as though they have an incredibly good handle on life. Keeping all of the balls safely in the air all of the time is often seen as one of the hallmarks of capability, drawing awestruck gasps of astonishment by those slightly intimidated by this seemingly effortless ability to manage life. An aura of busyness is an effective armor against intimacy, as people might be wary of "being a bother" and, similarly, might reason that the busy person's apparent lack of deeper connection is connected to the fact that "they're always on the go."

Appearances can be deceiving, and this is often the case with avoidant people. It's common for them to fit society's picture of the well-adjusted person, which again has the dual effect of creating an impression of being just fine while also keeping others at bay. You could think of it as war paint. Success is another arm of this—the aura of capability is enhanced by outward achievement, be that glowing exam results, the top job at work, or ownership of a big house.

Oddly enough, those who shun intimacy are often deeply fascinated with others: asking questions, listening carefully to answers, and generally seeming to engage closely. The effect? The appearance of being close to others, who are often left feeling swaddled in kindness without realizing the avoidant person has deflected any questions about themselves that might allow anyone to develop a closer friendship.

The Closeness Catch-22

Sabotaging relationships can be a defensive action to which avoiders resort. Behaviors such as deflecting conversation, being unavailable, or surrounding oneself with crowds of acquaintances are some of the ways that they might shut down a relationship before it has a chance to get off the ground. Some avoiders, however, actively crave closeness and will invest wholeheartedly in a relationship before their fear takes over and they quickly douse the flames of their enthusiasm with displays of coldness. These intense, short-term relationships can take many forms—the person with a string of romances, each definitely being "the one," a new best friend every month, or a fresh group of friends with whom they have so much in common. The act of sabotage comes in different guises too, including criticism, ignoring (blanking), sudden coldness, fight-picking, infidelity, and even disappearance.

For the person on the receiving end, sabotage can feel hurtful and utterly bewildering. Yet the avoidant person could be just as confused and dismayed by their own actions—they might not recognize that their need for closeness, once met, brings with it a deep-seated fear of being suffocated or abandoned.

DEALING WITH AN AVOIDER?

1. Don't Take It Personally

When another's behavior is hurting you, it can be useful to keep in mind that their actions stem from how they're feeling, not from anything that you've done.

Think about a time you've been at the receiving end of a close person's hurtful behavior. What are some possible reasons for their actions—what might have they been feeling? Why would they have behaved in this way?

....

....

....

....

....

....

2. Don't Mirror Their Behavior

As difficult as it is, remember that fear lies at the heart of intimacy avoidance. Aloofness, criticism, anger, or neediness will serve only to solidify fears of being overwhelmed or abandoned. Relationship-sabotaging actions are usually most noticeable when the person truly values that relationship. Their real selves will be most prominent when they're relaxed. If they say something that's untoward, don't be afraid to call them on it when they're in a more centered frame of mind.

Look to their actions over their words—how do they differ from each other?

....

....

....

....

....

....

3. Maintain Your Own Life

Being socially self-sufficient will make it easier to bear the avoidant person's sabotage mode, and it's also likely, somewhat paradoxically, to draw them back to you as they learn to trust that you won't lean too heavily on them.

A person who shies away from close connection can find it difficult talking about themselves. What gentle questions could you ask to encourage them to open up to you?

....

....

....

....

....

....

....

....

....

....

....

....

....

....

....

....

....

THINK YOU MIGHT BE THE AVOIDER?

1. Exercise Clarity about Your Past
Looking at previous events through clear eyes can be helpful in identifying current patterns. This might be safest in a therapeutic context.

Think about events from your past that could have contributed to your fear of intimacy and record them here.

....

....

....

....

....

....

....

....

2. Practice Self-Care
Being gentle with yourself and accepting that you're worthy of kindness will eventually help you be more receptive to others.

Repeat the following eight affirmations to yourself out loud daily. If you like, you can use these in conjunction with a 5- to 10-minute meditation:

- I accept myself exactly as I am now.
- I accept myself unconditionally.
- I accept love from myself.
- I am at peace with where I am.
- I embrace who I am.
- I am perfect, just as I am.
- I am creating my own love.
- I am enough.

3. Give It Time

Don't expect behavioral patterns to disappear overnight. Allowing yourself time and space for gradual changes will be far less threatening and more likely to be successful.

What changes could you make? List a few here. Work on one at a time, ticking them off as you go. Don't worry if it's taking longer than you expected to make headway; being aware of them will be useful in itself and is likely to spark unconscious change.

In All Modesty

Learning to graciously accept praise, instead of downplaying your successes, can help you feel more confident about yourself and your abilities.

Has someone ever complimented you on your appearance, only to be met by an embarrassed laugh and "Hardly—I look awful"? Or perhaps you've been introduced to someone as "a talented illustrator" and you've mumbled, "Oh, I draw a bit." In the workplace, when a manager congratulates you on a job well done, do you brush off the praise with "Well, everyone did a great job"? Although humility is a positive character trait (after all, self-importance rarely wins people over), there are situations where we're required to "sell ourselves." It's difficult to imagine a prospective employer being impressed by an interview statement such as "I guess I'm okay at accounting" or "I suppose I'm kind of a people person." So why, when it comes to situations where we're not actively required to self-promote yet still merit recognition for our talents or efforts, do so many of us deflect praise?

Accept Yourself

Lack of self-acceptance could be one reason. When people feel undeserving—also known as impostor syndrome—it can affect how they respond to recognition. Precisely why people feel this way might vary from individual to individual—yet doesn't everyone deserve positive feedback? Yes, it's good to temper a response with acknowledgment of other factors that might have played a role in your achievement (think, for instance, of awards acceptance speeches, where actors give credit to everyone who was a part of the moviemaking process), but that's not to say the achievement in question is not, at least in part, yours. In highlighting the input of others, it's important to ensure you're not rendering your own contributions invisible—or worthless.

Perfection Myth

Perfectionist tendencies can provide another inclination to dismiss praise—to accept recognition for something might cause the perfectionist to feel pressure, rather than pleasure. Was their achievement actually any good? And if it was, will they be expected to achieve it again? Just supposing they can't live up to that? Imagine, for example, being introduced as a marathon runner, but hastening to say, "Well, I've only done one, and it took me nearly five hours." Perhaps, also, we feel that our achievements fade into insignificance alongside other people's efforts, causing us to critique our own successes harshly.

Know Your Value

There are times when it's appropriate simply to smile and say thank you, without discussing relative merits. That said, there's no shame in accepting praise. Perhaps there'll be some who respond with jealousy, but consider the alternatives. When you don't claim your worth, you risk devaluing yourself in the eyes of others, as well as your own. However ambivalent you are about your own merit, there's a self-perpetuating danger in downplaying: you convince others you're nothing special, they treat you accordingly, and in turn, you become increasingly convinced that it's true. Keeping ambition and success under wraps also sends a message to others that these are things to be ashamed of, which sets a less-than-positive precedent for others in your realm of acquaintance.

Be Proud

Self-deprecation may be charming in some cases, as it's relatable and can also be humorous—the stuff of popular culture, sitcoms, and stand-ups. Context is key, however. Friends and family, for example, should ideally be able to celebrate each other's successes. In the workplace, we should be able to acknowledge our wins and simultaneously give credit to those who've played a role. The line is not always an easy one to draw. As a starting point, however, remember that there's a difference between being prideful and being proud.

HOW TO OWN RECOGNITION

Use these tips to learn how to graciously accept praise:

- When somebody gives you praise or acknowledges your efforts, imagine you're being given a physical gift, beautifully wrapped and boxed. You wouldn't bat such a present away or tell the giver that they should give it to someone else, would you? It's likely you'd accept it graciously.

- Taking yourself out of your own head and thinking about others can help with feelings of anxiety and lack of self-worth, so try to think about the other person's feelings or agenda. You might have done something which, to someone else, may be a goal. If you dismiss your achievement, how will that make them feel about themselves and their own prospects?

- If you're uncomfortable with attention, you can simply look the person in the eye, thank them, then deflect the focus from yourself by engaging with them on a related subject. An exchange could, for example, go along these lines:

  Person one: *Meredith tells me you're an incredible musician.*
  You: *Thank you, that's so kind. Do you play an instrument too?*

- Aim for a "happy high status," where you have presence and confidence, without being arrogant. It's where humble and powerful meet. Think in terms of "and" rather than "but": "Thank you, I enjoyed it and was grateful to be supported by a strong team. I will pass your feedback on to them, as well," instead of "Thanks, but it was the rest of the team really."

- Practice this affirmation: *I am a work in progress and I accept the good others see in me.*

- Accepting praise gets easier with practice. Remembering the nice things people have said about you and your achievements can help you to start seeing yourself in a more positive light.

RECEIVING A COMPLIMENT

Jot down compliments that people have paid you recently—it could be anything, from how nicely you dressed over the weekend to how well you executed a tricky project at work.

➤ ....

....

➤ ....

....

➤ ....

....

Reflect on how these compliments made you feel. Really focus on the emotions that cropped up. Were you proud? Embarrassed? Skeptical? A mixture? You can also write down what your response was to the praise, using as much detail as your memory allows.

....

....

....

....

....

....

....

....

....

If you felt negative emotions, try to get to the root of them. Why did you feel that way? Is it because you didn't feel worthy of praise? Is it because you didn't believe you were as good as the person said you were?

Explore your reaction and the reasons behind it.

....

....

....

....

....

....

....

....

Now think about how you can graciously accept this same compliment. Use some of the tips in the previous pages or create your own response.

....

....

....

....

....

....

....

....

Feed Your Senses

Flavor perception and experience of food is a huge part of everyday life, but it's only in recent years that the science labs and kitchens have come together to show enjoyment of food is more than taste buds alone. Using all the senses to make the most out of your culinary experiences is a mindful way to ground yourself to that very moment.

Professor Charles Spence, head of the Crossmodal Research Group at the University of Oxford, is responsible for carving the way for a new food revolution using a contemporary form of research known as gastrophysics. His groundbreaking work offers fresh insight into how all the senses interact during the process of eating. Through a series of studies, including some collaborations with British chef Heston Blumenthal at his Michelin-starred restaurant The Fat Duck, Professor Spence has revealed that when it comes to flavor perception, the shape, texture, color, sound, and smell of food all play an integral role.

"There is little that is more multisensory than flavor—it's one of the few experiences that really does engage all of our senses: sight, sound, smell, taste, touch, and even pain," says Professor Spence. "I was lucky enough to be introduced to Heston fifteen years ago and almost immediately realized the latest gastrophysics findings could be taken in tasty directions."

From using the sound of lapping waves and gull calls as diners ate a plate of oysters (which resulted in participants finding the shellfish considerably more gratifying than those listening to a soundtrack of farmyard chickens), to altering the lighting and giving restaurant-goers a piece of silk or sandpaper to hold during a course, Professor Spence has made it his mission to unveil the secrets of sensory seasoning. And thanks to his discoveries, cooking and dining can now be seen as a multisensual art, using stimuli to enhance and alter the flavor of food—without even tweaking an actual recipe.

As it turns out, the papillae on the tongue have a relatively limited role in picking up flavor, only transmitting the basics of sweet, sour, savory (umami), salt, and bitter to the brain without the nuances that make a meal. "Our experience of food is complex," says the professor. "As soon as we see food or drink, even if it's only an advert or picture, our brain can't help simulating the act of eating and drinking, and making predictions about what it will taste like and how much we'll enjoy it."

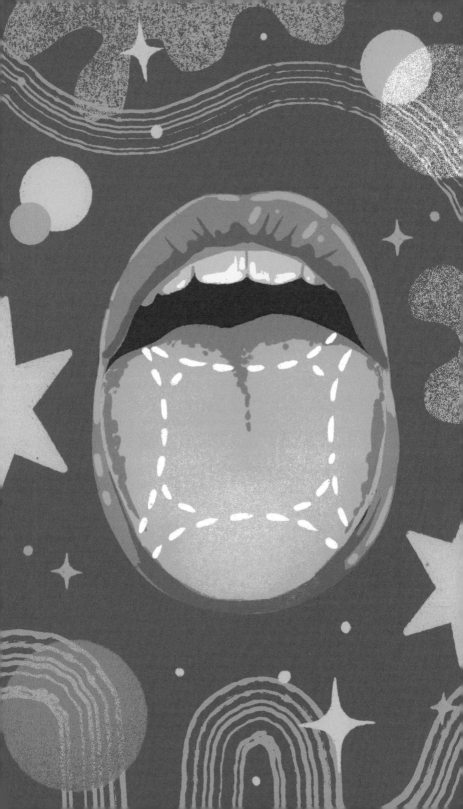

THE MEAL DEAL

Want to get the most out of your food? Then the dining experience must be considered as a whole. With simple changes to the presentation and the surrounding environment, you, too, can conduct gastrophysics experiments in the comfort of your home. With all sensory modalities working together in harmony, your relationship with food can then reach ambrosial heights—fans of great flavor will be able to treat themselves to a realm of dining of which they could previously only dream.

1. Playing with Food

Different textures, both within a meal and from outside sources while eating, have the ability to drastically alter expectations of how something should taste and, therefore, the way it does taste.

This can work simply by holding different textures in your hand as you eat or by introducing that texture to your lips and tongue through varied foodstuffs or textured cutlery. Although texture undoubtedly enhances and enriches certain tastes, it's also important not to overwhelm the senses, as this can be detrimental to flavor.

To Enhance Sweet Flavors

- Silky smooth textures are associated with sweetness. Some dessert brands even offer velvet or silk-covered chocolate pots, not just to be aesthetically pleasing but to trigger the mind into perceiving sweeter flavors.
- Soft and round food enhances the creamy aspects of a dish, which often goes hand in hand with sweetness.

To Enhance Salty Flavors

- Rough textures bring out salty flavors. Some recipes can forgo sodium entirely if you hold a piece of sandpaper as you eat.
- A crispy texture within food leads a person to expect either salty or fresh, depending on the visuals.

To Enhance Bitter Flavors

- Jagged shapes go hand in hand with bitter taste, so holding an angular object or eating something with edges will bring that flavor out.

To Enhance Umami (Savory) Flavors

- Umami is that protein flavor that goes a long way in making us feel full. Because it's so strongly associated with broiling, the texture that comes from this cooking technique helps to increase the umami flavor perception.

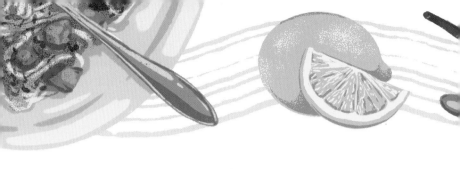

2. Entice Your Hunger

Who knew that visual hunger and digital satiation were things? Images of
beautifully portrayed, succulent food is, amazingly, enough to get those hunger
pangs going . . . and then satisfy them. Without so much as a single bite touching
your lips, nay, without the actual presence of physical food, your mind and body
can feel as though it has enjoyed the meal that you have merely laid eyes on in
photo-form. From design to lighting, colors to food placement, and choice of
crockery to table setting, all of these food-extrinsic considerations can make or
break a meal.

To Enhance Sweet Flavors

- The color red makes sweet flavors more intense. Inject some red into dining by
  using red lighting, red plates, and even red food, and you'll taste results.
- Don't want to use a red plate? Try a round white plate to boost the perception
  of sweet and creamy flavors.
- Serve food in a round shape on a round plate to boost the perception
  of sweetness.

To Enhance Salty Flavors

- The choice of cutlery has been shown to alter perceptions of salty flavors.
  Professor Spence discovered that cheese eaten from a knife tastes saltier than
  from a spoon or toothpick.
- Use the word salty on a menu to activate the same cognitive expectations as
  when a salty flavor is actually experienced in the mouth.

To Enhance Bitter Flavors

- As well as enhancing sweetness, the color red will lower your detection for the
  taste of bitterness.
- Hard-edged shapes make for a more bitter taste, so serve angular food if you
  want to bring this out.

To Enhance Umami Flavors

- Go for a thick sauce rather than a thin jus for a stronger umami flavor.

3. Listen Carefully

Despite often being neglected, audible alterations can have a big impact. "Sound really is the forgotten flavor sense," reveals Professor Spence. "Think about all those desirable attributes of food and drink that we love—the crispy, the crackly, the crunchy, the creamy, and the carbonated. All of these flavor sensations are influenced to a greater or lesser extent by what we hear when we eat. Beyond that, the background noise in many restaurants, or while dining in the air, can also suppress ability to taste."

To Enhance Sweet Flavors

- High-pitched music makes for a sweeter meal.
- Loud noise or music (80 decibels or above, the noise level of city traffic) can lead to greater enjoyment of sweet foods, theoretically because of a stress response within the body. However, it doesn't necessarily make sweet flavors more apparent. When there is a combination of flavors and you're aiming to bring sweetness out, low background noise (moderate conversation or a moderate rain shower) is preferable.
- Soft foods are associated with sweetness, so hearing the silence of putting a spoon into whipped cream or cutting through a velvety cake invites you to expect a sweet taste.

To Enhance Salty Flavors

- We expect crunchy foods to be either fresh or salty, depending on their appearance. Hearing an audible crunch enhances the perception of salt, so you can easily introduce a salty contrast to a meal by adding a crunchy element, such as toasted pecans on a pecan pie.

To Enhance Bitter Flavors

- Low-pitched sounds bring out the bitter taste in food.

To Enhance Umami Flavors

- Umami is the only flavor that is enhanced by very loud noise, whereas all other tastes are suppressed. This might explain why a Bloody Mary is the most frequently ordered drink on flights—it actually tastes better when accompanied by a loud engine.

Be the Change

Creating a cleaner, greener world where humans can live in healthy harmony with nature starts with the realization that everyone can make a difference to the planet through conscious lifestyle choices. And living a life close to nature, while taking care of this important part of our world, allows us to truly thrive.

Do you feel a sense of helplessness when you hear about the pollution of land, water, and air; deterioration of urban and rural environments; threats to wildlife and their habitats; soil erosion; deforestation; and seas full of plastic? The list of problems seems endless, and the solutions out of reach. Environmental changes have consequences for everyone, but it's easy to feel disempowered and to believe that individual action won't make a difference. There is, however, much that can be done on a personal level to bring about change. It just requires greener everyday choices and rekindling a connection with nature.

Connected to Nature

Andy Goldsworthy is a sculptor, photographer, and environmentalist who creates work for urban and rural settings. "We often forget we are nature," he says. "Nature is not something separate from us. So, when we say that we have lost our connection to nature, we've lost our connection to ourselves." It makes sense that nature-friendly choices effectively mean being kinder to one's self and each other. Each small action can make a difference and inspires and influences others to make greener choices, too. The poet Ralph Waldo Emerson once said, "The creation of a thousand forests is in one acorn." When we each take greater responsibility for the way we live, we plant a seed and become part of the solution that will benefit the planet, our communities, and ourselves.

Going Green

Living a greener life might seem daunting at first, and some people are discouraged because they think it's inconvenient, takes too much effort, and is too costly. But there are many personal advantages to being Earth-friendly alongside the obvious environmental benefits. For example, choosing food and products that are organic and free of chemicals is known to be better for well-being, while reducing consumption of energy and water results in lower bills.

Small Steps

If being the change you wish to see in the world seems overwhelming, focus on doing what feels doable and actionable right now. Make one ethical choice today, and then another tomorrow. Look at the personal and wider benefits of how your choices make a difference. The key is to start from where you are, with what you have, and be at peace with the knowledge that you're doing something, no matter how small or insignificant it may seem.

There are many inspiring people who are "being the change they wish to see in the world." It's through individual and community, grassroots initiatives, and action that we can restore the necessary ecological balance and create healthier lives in harmony with nature.

SPEND WISELY

When you choose to invest in ethical and Earth-friendly ventures, you play a part by influencing the wider industry to move to eco-friendly practices. Before purchasing, follow the money trail and research how companies use their profits. Where possible, let your green values guide your spending.

- **Conserve energy and water.** Turn off your computer, lights, and other electrical devices when not in use. Lower the thermostat on your hot water and central heating. Repair leaks or dripping taps. Install water-saving toilets and shower heads. Only use the washing machine or dishwasher with a full load.

- **Go organic.** Research the ingredients that go into your food, personal care, and household cleaning products. Shop locally if possible and support organic farmers when you can.

- **Switch to a green energy company.** Choose suppliers who use renewable sources for gas and electric.

- **Reuse, recycle, and upcycle.** Choosing recycled products means a reduction in the demand for raw materials in the form of forests, metals, fuels, and chemical pollutants. It also means less goes to a landfill.

- **Grow your own food.** Be creative—use your backyard, balcony, or windowsills to grow tasty, fresh, and nutritious vegetables, salad greens, fruit, or herbs. Where possible, share gardening space with other members of your community. It doesn't cost much to grow your own food, and it'll help to reduce grocery bills.

- **Carry a shopping bag.** Say no to plastic bags and excessive packaging. Use your own bags, boxes, or cartons when shopping for food and other items.

- **Travel green.** Use public transport where practical. If you're buying a car, choose one that is fuel-efficient or uses renewable energy. Consider carpooling for commuting to work. If making a shorter journey, think about walking or cycling instead.

- **Go vegetarian or vegan—or just cut down on meat.** There are many exciting, nutritious plant-based recipes out there.

- **Choose good threads.** Support ethical, fair-trade companies that use eco-friendly materials, like organic cotton, hemp, bamboo, or flax. For a bargain and something unique, try thrift stores.

- **Stand up for wildlife and the environment.** Become knowledgeable about issues that matter to you. Support campaigns that focus on protecting natural habitats and wildlife.

- **Carry out conservation work.** Support tree, wildflower, and hedgerow planting. Clean up litter. Participate in Earth-friendly community initiatives.

- **Create your own Earth-friendly venture.** Do you have an ethical business idea? Be inspired by nature and follow your heart. Your ideas might pave the way for a greener world.

MY ECO-WEEK

With some of the ideas from the previous page, you can commit to making a few eco-friendly choices throughout the week, some new, some replacing old habits. This might include having a meat-free day, shopping at a zero-waste store where you fill up your own containers, or cycling to work instead of taking the car. Spend some time in the morning to write down your intentions for the day, and on Sunday, use the space to explore your reflections and thoughts, jotting down what worked well (and perhaps what didn't), as well as how you might bring more green into your life the week after. If the exercise works well, could you make this a weekly practice?

Monday

....

....

....

....

....

....

Tuesday

....

....

....

....

....

....

Wednesday

Thursday

Friday

Saturday

Sunday

....

....

....

....

....

....

....

....

....

WORK IT OUT

- If something didn't work well for you, think about why that was. Was it due to convenience? Habit? Or is there genuinely no space for the swap in your life? If it's a case of getting used to the eco-alternative, consider trying again or tweaking your method slightly.

- If something worked really well, great! Is there a way to take it even further?

- It's also important to remember not to feel too guilty and just do the best you can. Making small changes is better than not doing anything at all.

Enter the Labyrinth

For a mindful meditation, use the labyrinth pictured above or on the next page and trace the route with your finger.

Not to be confused with a maze, with its cul-de-sacs, multiple entrances, and blind choices, a labyrinth has only one convoluted path leading to a central point that is always visible. The path may meander, shifting in unexpected ways. Often it seems to steer you away from your goal, but ultimately, surrendering yourself to it, you will find your way through.

CIRCLE OF CALM

Mindfully gliding a finger through a labyrinth requires preparation. Before entering, settle into yourself. Notice where your breath enters and leaves; don't try to alter it, just observe for a few mindful moments. Decide what you want from your experience. Perhaps you have something you'd like to let go of, a burning question you need answered, some creative inspiration, or simply the peace that meditative practice can bring. Frame your intention clearly.

- Enter the labyrinth. Your movements should be mindful and steady, slowing the mind and allowing you to move from thinking to tapping into intuition. At times when emotions are high, you may find a faster pace allows you to release any pent-up feelings.

- The key is to have your mind and body in the same place and not rush forward to the end of the labyrinth and the tasks you need to do later or reflect back on earlier issues. If you notice yourself doing this, gently tug your attention back to the feel of your fingers as you trace the twining trail. Release your intentions and immerse yourself in the experience.

- As you make your convoluted journey through the labyrinth, the babble of your mind may begin to quiet, mirroring the empty space at its center. When you arrive at the center, allow yourself just to be. This is a pure void in which to do absolutely nothing. When we finally yield to stillness and silence, we are often rewarded with the purest of inspiration, profound wisdom, or a moment of blissful serenity.

- Leaving the labyrinth is as important as entering. When you are ready, trace your path out as steadily and mindfully as you entered. Accept with gratitude that which you have released and gained, and be receptive to anything that may still arise.

- Before you cross the threshold of the labyrinth, pause to check in with yourself and your feelings. Do you feel ready to reenter the everyday world? Take a moment to think about how you might use what you have gained from the experience.

start
here

Don't Forget to Write

When relentlessly racing from one task to another, it can be surprisingly easy to lose sight of who you are and what you believe is truly important. Taking the time to note down your thoughts can help you to pause, find your center, and reconnect with your inner self.

Have you ever been busy with work, socializing, responsibilities and life in general, and then suddenly felt disoriented, as though you've spent so much time connecting with the outside world that you've lost touch with your internal one? Feeling separate from your self can result in a sense of alienation.

It can help to think of your emotional, inner life like a kind of garden. It needs constant tending and pruning to keep it all in order. Neglect can see it grow wild and into a state of disarray. And the longer you leave it untended, the bigger emotions and thoughts have to be to attract your attention.

With your inner self in confusion, you may struggle to navigate the outer world. With no clear sense of what you think and feel, decision-making can become difficult. You might have a million things to do but struggle to know what to do first, or have several creative ideas and not be sure of where to start. Losing that inner compass can set you adrift.

Return to Yourself

Writing is one method you could use to get back to being you and start listening to yourself again, gently noticing and acknowledging your emotions. It can be a way of sorting through tangled thoughts and finding clarity.

During busy periods, writing might be the type of thing you avoid, because you think that you don't have time for it. But why not take a different approach? Keep this journal in your desk drawer, take it out, and write for just ten minutes a day—or however long you can spare to accomplish the odd bit of mental pruning. Just like gardening, short bursts of activity often add up to significant progress. After these mini writing sessions, you can return to the world with a better sense of self, more able to approach things from a place of perspective and meaning.

FIVE WAYS TO FIND YOURSELF

As you work through these exercises, write down the first thoughts that come to mind. Try not to second-guess or think, "Oh, that's not right." Acknowledging whatever comes to mind, even when it seems nonsensical or unimportant, is a way to train yourself to listen and stay connected. It's only through listening to your self that you can traverse your mind's chatter and find the gold. Before trying these exercises, you might want to spend a short time sitting quietly and focusing on your breathing. Meditation can help the process of getting back to yourself by putting you more in touch with your thoughts. Guided meditation can be helpful when you've been busy.

1. Brain Dump

In the space below, draw an oval or brain shape. Inside it, write down the contents of your mind, all those thoughts and feelings that you've been neglecting. It could be single words such as "sadness," "frustration," "work," "deadlines," or "anxiety." Let the thoughts come fast and commit them to paper. Then, in the space on the right, add single sentences to expand upon what you've written, or anything that springs to mind about what's going on inside your head. Feel free to get creative and use colored pens to reflect different thoughts and moods. This can be a powerful exercise in itself, helping you to express what's going on for you and allowing you to feel more connected with yourself.

2. Free Writing

If you have more time, choose one thought or feeling—perhaps the one that seems most pressing. Then, using the space below, write down whatever comes to mind about this topic. Simply listen to your thoughts and note them on the page. Don't feel like you have to stay focused on that one particular feeling or thought; just keep jumping from one to another, and trust that your mind is telling you what it needs to.

As you write, notice how your body feels. Do you become tense while you write about a certain emotion? Focus on relaxing and then keep writing out your thoughts. Take note of your breathing. Is it shallow or deep? Bringing some focused attention to your body and breath as you write can help you to stay connected with yourself.

3. The Anti-to-do List
Does your to-do list seem like a constant whisper in the back of your mind? Something that reminds you of yet another thing you're supposed to be doing every time you try to relax? Does that to-do list come with anxiety, drudgery, exhaustion, or resentment?

For this exercise, bring out your to-do list and rewrite it in the space below. Each time you note down a task, leave a big space to express your feelings about it. Allow those whispering thoughts to come to life and let them out on the page.

....

....

....

....

....

....

....

....

....

....

....

....

....

....

....

4. Look Deeper
Asking a few questions can help you to reach yourself.

What is your mind trying to tell you?

....

....

....

....

....

What are you struggling to hear?

....

....

....

....

....

What does your self need right now?

....

....

....

....

....

....

5. A New Location

Sometimes, changing the scenery can be a holiday from the everyday and a trip back to the self. Find a quiet space that is inspiring, rather than full of noise and distractions, and sit with a tea, this journal, and a pen. Or write in nature, a garden, or park. Even something as simple as a long bath can bring the stillness you need to create that escape from the busyness of everyday life.

Look around you. What do you see? Jot down thoughts that spring to mind.

....

....

....

....

....

....

....

Has something brightened your day? Why should you savor moments like this?

....

....

....

....

....

....

....

....

How to Embrace Meditation

Meditation can be useful for moving from surviving to thriving, but there are many reasons why establishing a regular practice can be a struggle. Here we tackle some of the most common barriers so you might feel encouraged to give it another chance.

I Can't Make My Mind Go Blank or Empty, However Much I Try

You'll be glad to know you can stop trying right now because meditation isn't about emptying your mind or making it go blank (it's pretty impossible to do this). When you meditate, you can focus on one thing, such as the breath or repeating a mantra, or you can shift attention intentionally from one sense to another. You're not thinking of everything at the same time; you're being intentional and focusing on one thing at a time. It's often simplest to focus on the breath because it's always with you.

My Mind Won't Stay on One Thing. A Million Thoughts Pop into My Head, Which Lead to Another and Another . . .

While the intention is to focus attention on one thing, the mind is going to wander off to other thoughts over and over again. It just will, so there's no need to get annoyed with yourself, think you're bad at meditating, or that you're doing it wrong. It's called meditation practice for a reason. In time and with practice, the mind is trained to stay focused for longer. Noticing your mind has wandered off to other thoughts is part of meditating and shows you're increasing your awareness because you've noticed your mind drifting.

Meditation Makes Me Sleepy (When I Don't Want to Sleep)

It could be that you need more sleep, but there are other reasons why you feel like nodding off when meditating. The time of day can have an impact. Many people feel more awake in the morning and find it easier to meditate then, rather than in the afternoon when you can have an energy slump. A relaxed sitting posture can contribute to an urge to fall asleep, too, so take a look at how you sit when you meditate. Ideally you want to be in a firm chair, with both feet flat on the ground and your back a little away from the seatback, so it's self-supporting but not stiff. Work with the furniture you have and with what feels comfortable for you, and aim for an alert, wakeful posture.

Sitting Still in Silence Makes Me Anxious. Is There a Way to Meditate While Moving?

When being busy is your norm and there's lots going on around you, it can feel alien, uncomfortable even, to be in silence and not moving. First, rather than closing your eyes, you can simply lower your gaze to a spot on the ground in front of you. Listening to a guided meditation, where a voice is talking you through the meditation step by step, can help with the issue of silence and make it feel like you're with a friend (as long as you like the person's voice, of course). If being still is an issue, you could try mindful movement. Chi kung (qi gong) is an ancient Chinese healing exercise that integrates movement, breathing, and intention. It's a simple sequence of movements that allow you to focus on your breath while moving your body.

If I Could Meditate without Having to Schedule Extra Time in My Day I'd Be More Likely to Try It

While formal meditation practice in a peaceful place where you're unlikely to be disturbed for a period of time is more beneficial, you could practice a more informal, mindful form of meditation on the go. For example, when you're on a train or bus, you could bring your attention to your breath, where you feel it most clearly as you inhale and exhale. Or you could take a few moments at work to focus on an object on your desk, noticing its color, shape, and texture. As you walk down the street or through a park you could focus on the sounds you hear or the sensation of each foot as it makes contact with the ground. What's important is that you take your experience for what it is, without judging or making up a story. You're in that moment, focusing on the form of an object, the feel of your breath, or your feet on the ground just as it is, there and then.

"Meditation is not a way of making your mind quiet. It's a way of entering into the quiet that's already there—buried under the 50,000 thoughts the average person thinks every day."

Deepak Chopra

Meditation Takes Up Too Much Time—I'm Too Busy for It

Meditation isn't something to which you need to devote great chunks of your day (or night). More is better, but you could meditate in just a few minutes when you're at work or out and about, as well as sitting in a more formal practice. But even this could be five or ten minutes—work with however much time is available. There's a wealth of research that shows how beneficial meditating each day is for your well-being and mental health, so you might discover that scheduling a few minutes in your diary to slow your body and mind, focus your attention on one thing, and take a few breaths is very much worth it for the feeling of calm you gain. Meditating isn't all or nothing. If you meditate every day that's great and if you do it once in a while that's good, too. Just as we have a new day every twenty-four hours, so we have a fresh opportunity to meditate every time we make that decision.

Focusing on My Breath Makes Me Self-Conscious and Uncomfortable

There are several different ways to meditate—focusing on the breath is only one of them. It's popular because your breath is always with you. Alternatively, you could do a body scan where you bring your attention to your feet and slowly work your way up your body, focusing on each part (not judging or trying to change it) one at a time, until you reach the top of your head.

Or you could try a sitting meditation where you focus on how your body feels sitting in the chair, then the sounds you can hear, then the feelings you're experiencing, and then noticing thoughts come and go in your mind. There's loving-kindness meditation where you repeat a series of words to send compassion to yourself and others. Choiceless awareness meditation involves observing your mind wandering where it pleases—from your breath to your thoughts to feelings to sound—and noticing each movement and its flow from one to the next. Mindful movement, as we've already discussed, is also beneficial. All meditation asks you to be in the moment, without judgment, just as you are. Try out the different forms to see what you feel comfortable with and perhaps even mix up your practice so that you don't get bored.

YOU ARE NOT YOUR THOUGHTS

Struggling to stay focused? Learn to let go of distractions.

- Every time you realize you're distracted, bring your attention back to whatever is the focus of the meditation.

- You can gain a little distance from your mind's wanderings by labeling them each time you realize your mind has meandered, as "thinking" or "feeling."

- Don't judge or get angry with yourself.

- Simply say "oh, thinking" or "ah, feeling" and then bring your attention back to the focus of the meditation.

- Do this every time your mind wanders.

- It doesn't matter how many times your thoughts drift off—what is important is that you notice and come back to what you're focusing on for the meditation.

> "Always be a first-rate version of yourself and not a second-rate version of someone else."

Judy Garland

Be the Real Deal

Take these steps to start thriving as your true, authentic self.

The concept of authenticity has generated arguments since the earliest civilizations. The ancient Greeks, including the polymath Aristotle, were as concerned with the idea of living truthfully as many people are today, bemoaning the superficial electronic lives we all lead. So, how does a person live authentically? The French philosopher Jean-Paul Sartre, writing in the 1940s, believed it was by "one choosing the freedom of following one's own path in life." An existentialist, Sartre explored the essence of what it was to be human. Authenticity, for him, was about being who you wanted to be, rather than giving in to the push and pull of the expectations of others.

Live By Your Values

Chris Cowie, philosophy professor at Durham University in England, agrees in part. He describes authenticity as "being reliant on one's own values when choosing how to live—and so, taking responsibility for one's life, rather than being reliant on the values of others." Aristotle thought one of the best ways to adopt appropriate values for the self was to identify how they played out in others. Chris expands on this, explaining that while solely relying on others' values to make decisions is irresponsible, identifying with their positive values can be responsible.

The key is in choosing to embody a value because you want to rather than because someone else happens to do it. Imagine, for example, a friend gives you a present tailored to your interests. It could be a basket filled with your favorite treats, a mixtape of songs you love, or a notebook of precious photos. This would suggest their values included kindness and compassion, and you might choose to embody these traits yourself by doing something equally as special for people you care about.

Be Yourself

It's important to note that electing to live authentically might not feel great at first. It could involve challenging—and sometimes ignoring—what other people think you should be doing. In fact, Sartre's beliefs are connected to a concept called radical freedom—the notion that it's terrifying to be yourself. Could you follow a path no one has paved out before? This fear can extend to becoming or being the person you want to be, rather than the one society might like you to be. Either way, no one should feel pushed into following a well-beaten track; neither should they feel the need to be different for the sake of it. The important thing is to reach out and grab those things that are appropriate for you and to express yourself in a way that feels natural. This is a vital aspect of living authentically, and everyone will experience it in their own way.

Follow the impulse within you—bake a cake, take some photos, draw. Maybe you love nothing better than dancing, or maybe you enjoy reading, walking, or gardening. Following these impulses makes you who you are. For some, it might feel self-indulgent to do what you love. But this isn't the case. If you take the body's lead, it's natural. When your feet are tired, for example, you might put them up, while if your limbs ache, you might have a long soak in a hot bath full of healing salts. Just as you follow your body's needs, be led by the needs of the mind. Whether you want to meditate quietly or sing loudly, visit a friend, or be on your own, go for a walk in the forest or take in the sights of the city, follow that impulse. Why? Because that's authentic living.

Moral Dimension

No one can tell you how to live authentically—that would be inauthentic—but possibilities can be offered. In his essay "Existentialism Is a Humanism," Sartre relates an anecdote about when he was approached by a former student who was plagued by a moral dilemma and wanted advice on which path to take. The student, living in 1940s France, was stuck between a rock and a hard place: should he join many of his countrymen in the fight against the Nazis or stay at home with his mother, who was mourning the death of his brother in the war?

Sartre said he couldn't give any advice—only the student could arrive at the solution to the dilemma. And this should be based on what the young man wanted to do rather than what he felt he ought to do. In this way, he would be choosing the correct path, the one that felt authentic to him.

IDENTIFY YOUR CORE VALUES

Taking responsibility for your life means not being reliant on the values of others. To do this, it's first helpful to identify what your core values are. Can you pin down what is meaningful to you? Coming up with a list of values can be challenging. Honesty, kindness, community, freedom—what is most important to you?

Without thinking too much, write your response to the following questions. Jot down as much or as little as you feel you want to. For each, imagine having, doing, or being those things in as much detail as possible.

1. What Do You Have/Want to Have That's Important to You?

....

....

....

What would you see, hear, and feel?

....

....

....

What's so good about it?

....

....

....

What would it give you?

....

....

....

2. What Do You Want to Do?

....

....

....

....

....

....

What would you see, hear, and feel?

....

....

....

What's so good about it?

....

....

....

What would it give you?

....

....

....

3. Who Do You Want to Be?

....

....

....

....

....

....

What would you see, hear, and feel?

....

....

....

What's so good about it?

....

....

....

What would it give you?

....

....

....

4. What's Important to You?

Look at your responses to the questions on the previous page. What's the motivation behind each of your desires? There could be many different reasons. For example, wanting to volunteer for a charity could be about making a difference (contribution), meeting new people (connection), or, if you are volunteering abroad, you might be interested in travel (adventure). Identifying what's important to you in your choices can give insight into your unique ethos. Write down these motivations, using the values on the list below to help you. It's in no way exhaustive, so feel free to add more.

Examples of Core Values

Achievement	Faith	Optimism
Adventure	Fame	Peace
Authenticity	Fun	Popularity
Authority	Growth	Power
Balance	Happiness	Recognition
Boldness	Honesty	Reputation
Challenge	Humor	Respect
Citizenship	Influence	Security
Community	Justice	Self-respect
Compassion	Kindness	Service
Competence	Knowledge	Spirituality
Contribution	Leadership	Stability
Creativity	Learning	Status
Curiosity	Love	Success
Determination	Loyalty	Trustworthiness
Fairness	Openness	Wisdom

....

....

....

....

....

....

5. Assess Your Values

Now review the list. Notice any values that recur. The ones that appear most frequently are your core values—usually, there'll be three or four. Using a scale from zero to ten, assess the prevalence of each value in your life at the moment. If, say, contribution is at the top of your core values list, but scores only four on your scale, then it's likely that you might feel more fulfilled by bringing into your life tasks or projects where you're helping people or places. Usually, scores of less than seven indicate that the things you hold dear, or are most important to you, are not being reflected enough in your daily life. Putting them at the forefront of your mind will help you to make decisions and set goals that are more closely aligned to how you'd like your life to be.

"I am only one, but I am one. I can't do everything, but I can do something. The something I ought to do, I can do. And by the grace of God, I will."

Edward Everett Hale

Internal Affairs

Conflicting personal desires and needs may at first glance seem innocuous, but they can sap time and energy. If we learn how to resolve them, however, it's possible to move from surviving to thriving.

They're common scenarios: you want to go out with friends, but at the same time you need to stay in and save money; a work project requires that you stay late in the office, but you'd really like to leave on time to make your gym class; you have a list of household chores as long as your arm, but you also want to go out for a leisurely stroll in the winter sunshine to boost your sense of well-being. These competing needs and desires might at first resemble a harmless, superficial mental tug of war, but they go deeper and can affect your time and energy.

WHAT DO YOU WANT?

It all comes down to values—the things you believe to be important in life and into which you are willing to put time and energy. They form the basis of decision-making behavior. These values are useful when decisions are simple and clear, but they can be less helpful when trying to decide between two concerns of similar importance.

When you are focused on achieving one particular goal—for example, achieving good grades in your exams—nothing else gets in the way. But when goals are less clear and there are multiple aims, it gets messy and can cause anxiety, stress, and exhaustion. For this reason, it's important to be able to easily decipher between conflicting priorities to remain productive and efficient.

Before taking steps to achieve this balance, you need to identify your goals, work out which ones are clashing, and determine if they're as important as another. Try the following five-step plan to help resolve internal conflicts.

1. Stop Ignoring It

You cannot resolve anything that you don't consciously acknowledge. Sometimes when people come up against something they don't like or aren't happy with, their first response is to ignore it in the hope it will go away. But internal conflicts won't. The most common reason for ignoring the problem is because people don't feel they have the energy, time, or capability to do something about it. Instead, they push the conflicts deeper down and allow them to take root further in the mind. The first step to overcoming this habit is to treat the mind and body as you would treat someone else. Listen carefully to what they truly want and take conscious steps to eradicate the problem from the source.

If you feel unhappy about an area of your life but tell yourself "It's not that bad," this can be a sign that you're denying your desires. Try to be honest with yourself. How often do these feelings come about? How do you feel afterward?

....

....

....

....

....

....

2. Decide Which Goal Takes Priority Today

If deadlines are looming, then the overriding priority should be to get on top of your workload, and all your actions should lead to that end goal. If you want to concentrate on your health, then doing exercise and eating well should take precedence. If it's not practical to focus an entire day on one of these goals, then split your time and do a couple of hours studying before going to the gym and then return to your work. This will allow you to address both goals and help to keep you motivated and engaged. It's important to think consciously about these choices and their impact.

My goal today is:

....

....

....

....

....

....

Actions to take:

....

....

....

....

....

....

....

....

3. Learn to Say No

Most people like to honor all of their conflicting priorities all of the time, but this isn't possible. Every now and then it's necessary to assess goals and sometimes this involves saying no to something you believe you want. It's not always easy, but once you've mastered it, saying no can help you keep a clear head. Declining a post-work beer with colleagues when you want to go to the gym might be fine, but turning down extra office hours to spend time with your family might seem harder. It's important to understand that needs cannot be met every time.

A common German saying is "the practice makes the master," and this is true when it comes to internal conflicts. The more you learn to prioritize and say no to factors that try to get in the way of your end goals, the easier it will become.

Here are a few tips for learning to say no.

- Try to keep in mind the reason you're saying no.

- Be honest. Say that you appreciate the kind offer, but you don't have the time.

- Realize that you're turning down a request, not a person.

- Remember that you and your time are valuable—by saying no, you are choosing your own opinion.

- Don't over-apologize.

- Don't delay your response if you're sure you don't want to do it; it will only prolong the stress.

4. Create Rhythm Rather Than Balance

Just like an old-fashioned set of scales, life will never be perfectly balanced. Instead, it's important to plan your week around your priorities. Create routines you can stick to, with space for last-minute changes or emergencies. For example, deciding on set mornings or evenings to go to the gym can be a good idea, leaving other evenings free to relax or be with family. Having set plans can actually prevent you from feeling tied down too much.

Creating routines can be hard for those who enjoy going with the flow and take life in their stride. However, rather than impose a strict timetable, the purpose here is to find a rhythm that works for you by eliminating your conflicting priorities to find peace and calm in day-to-day life. This is a step that should be taken slowly, so instead of changing everything at once, try to alter one aspect initially and let it settle before moving on to the next one.

What important action could you create a routine for this week?

....

....

....

....

....

....

How will you fit it into your schedule?

....

....

....

....

....

....

....

5. Be Persistent

Sometimes, when you are changing aspects of your life and you hit a bad day when not everything goes according to plan, it's easy to feel demotivated and give up on end goals. Don't allow this to happen. Everyone has good and bad days. You might miss that gym class or slip behind on a project, but this doesn't mean you should give up. If you truly want something, you will need to stick to it through thick and thin while reminding yourself of the end goal and its associated rewards. Internal conflicts are part of life and it's nearly impossible to solve every one of them, but if you strive to limit their effects it can lead to a less stressful, more relaxed, and happier life, where decision-making is better informed and sleep comes more easily.

To keep track of your progress toward a goal, set up a reward system for yourself. Record your goals here and choose a reward for each milestone you accomplish on the way to your ultimate goal.

Ultimate goal:

....

....

....

First milestone:

....

....

....

....

Reward:

....

....

....

....

Second milestone:

....

....

....

....

Reward:

....

....

....

Third milestone:

....

....

....

Reward:

....

....

....

Neck Pain?

It may be commonplace, but that doesn't mean you have to suffer—simple yogic exercises can act as preventative measures against many everyday aches and strains, allowing you to thrive through a range of motion.

Delicate, elegant, versatile—whether displaying a piece of jewelry, spritzed with a scent, or shielded from the elements by a scarf—the neck is one of the most vulnerable parts of the body. In some cultures it's a symbol of beauty, wealth, and status, such as for the Kayan people of northern Thailand, where girls as young as five years old are fitted with brass jewelry that elongates their necks. The longer it is, the more attractive to the beholder.

Yet the neck also carries a big responsibility, quite literally, with the average human head weighing approximately 9–11 pounds (4–5 kg). This means a lifetime of supporting approximately 8 percent of the body's weight, which is heavy work. So it's little surprise that many people experience a literal pain in the neck from time to time. Fortunately, yoga offers some soothing solutions that can help to take care of this precious piece of anatomy.

Pillar of Support

The neck is made up of a complex range of bones, muscles, ligaments, tendons, nerves, and blood vessels, all working together to enable a range of movement from the forward flexion of nodding the head to extension, which allows the chin to protrude forward; side flexion, which lets you drop an ear toward the shoulder, as well as turning and circling the head. Swiss-based physiotherapist Monique Sanders explains, "The neck is the most movable part of the spinal cord, most of the time making a combination of these movements. Like all mammals, we have seven cervical vertebrae. The upper three move differently to the others, stabilizing the skull on the neck, while the others are supported by a lot of muscles that literally pull your head to your chest—at the front, sides, and back."

A Real Pain in the Neck

Neck pain can be debilitating, yet is also common. Worldwide estimates of its prevalence vary wildly, ranging from 17 to 75 percent, largely because of the difficulty in measuring when it happens and the vague nature of the problem. With a wide range of triggers—from a seemingly innocuous turn of the head, to carrying heavy bags and chronic issues resulting from habitual patterns—the effects of neck pain can be long-lasting, often causing significant disruption to everyday life. Increased reliance on technology is a major culprit—for example, leaning forward over a smartphone is said to increase the load on the neck and upper back muscles fivefold. More serious illnesses and diseases can also affect the neck—such as osteo- and rheumatoid arthritis.

Stress and its effects are another cause of neck pain, as explained by Monique, "People who experience emotional or physical stress will feel this in the neck first. We don't store deep emotions in our neck, but we do put our momentum stress there and headaches often occur because of tensed neck muscles."

Prevention Is Better Than Cure

Monique's advice? "Start stretching—soft movements are key. Without this, neck pain can become chronic." Maintaining healthy posture is also key to preventing neck pain. A good start is by becoming aware of the neck's position in relation to the rest of the body, taking care to keep the shoulders relaxed and the head vertically aligned with the spine. Avoid slouching forward or leaning to one side—both of which cause the delicate muscles of the neck to work extra hard to keep the head in place, leading to tension, pain, and, in more serious cases, numbness or tingling.

How Can Yoga Help?

When practiced in a conscious, mindful way that works within the safe limits of the body, yoga is a great way to keep the complex structure of the neck healthy. The combination of postures, movement, and breathing techniques complement each other to strengthen, lengthen, and mobilize—enhancing bodily awareness, improving posture, and relieving stress. Andrea, a fifty-year-old pediatric nurse, lived with pain in her neck and shoulders for many years. "It affected my posture and how comfortable I was while relaxing. I found it hard to sit with my head unsupported as it made my neck ache." She eventually turned to yoga in an attempt to find some relief, with great results. "I'm more aware of my posture when sitting, moving, and standing, I feel I know how to counteract any 'bad' postures I've had during the day."

As Andrea attests there are many positives to be gained by the introduction of a regular yoga practice, from the physical benefits of improved flexibility and strength to mental and emotional advantages, including lower stress levels and improved emotional resilience. "My body definitely feels stronger but yoga has helped mentally, just as much as physically. When I'm on the mat, I can almost forget all that's bothered me during the day or week."

The great thing is that even a short and simple routine practiced regularly can produce wonderful results. And this can all start by standing tall.

As with all forms of movement, take great care to move within the limits of your body and stop immediately if any pain is experienced. If you feel restricted mobility or ongoing pain in your neck, it's important to see your physician.

FOUR WAYS TO RELEASE TENSION

These exercises form part of the *Pawanmuktasana I* series, which is great for releasing tension and improving coordination. It's a good alternative for when more vigorous forms of exercise are not recommended and can be particularly helpful for those with arthritis or rheumatism. Move through the exercises slowly, gently, and mindfully, maintaining a rhythm of long, slow, deep breathing.

Start in a comfortable seated position—this can be on the floor or in a chair—and take a couple of minutes to relax your shoulders and tune into any sensations in your neck before beginning. Visualize a thread passing through your upper body—from the base of your spine, through your neck, and up through the crown of your head. Rest your hands on your lap and close your eyes if this feels comfortable; alternatively soften your gaze to a spot ahead of you.

1. Forward Flexing

- Drop your chin down toward your chest as far as is comfortable, noticing any sensations of stretching and loosening in the muscles of the back of your neck and across your shoulders.

- Return your head to the starting position, allowing the "thread" to create lightness in your upper body and lengthening your neck as the crown of your head lifts toward the sky.

- Alternate between the flexing and lifting movements, exhaling down and inhaling up.

- Repeat ten times.

2. Side Flexing

- Flex your left ear down toward your left shoulder as far as is comfortable, noticing any sensations of stretching and loosening of the muscles in the right side of your neck and top of your right shoulder. Keep your shoulders relaxed and level. Do not lift your shoulder up toward your ear.

- Slowly return your head to the start position.

- Repeat on your right side.

- Alternate sides, exhaling down and inhaling up to the center.

- Repeat ten times on each side.

3. Half Circles

- Drop your chin down toward your chest, continuing to half-circle your head to the left and lift and raise your chin until your head is looking over your left shoulder.

- Slowly retrace your movement through the center, continuing to repeat on your right side.

- Alternate the half circles from side to side, exhaling down and inhaling up. Do not move your head backward.

- Repeat ten times on each side.

4. Rotations

- Turn your head to the left—keeping your shoulders facing forward—until your head is looking over your left shoulder.

- Slowly retrace the movement through the center, continuing to rotate over to the right side.

- Alternate sides, exhaling to look over your shoulder and inhaling to the center.

- Repeat ten times on each side.

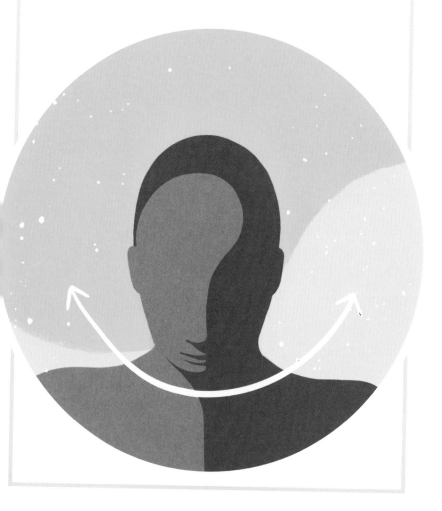

Guilty Conscience

You've committed no crime. You've caused no upset with an ill-judged remark. You haven't even let anyone down. Exactly why, then, do you feel guilty?

"The fact of having committed a specified or implied offence or crime" and "a feeling of having committed wrong or failed in an obligation." This is how the Oxford English Dictionary defines guilt. It's a tricky customer, often unseen and frequently unrecognized. Yet it can be responsible for a wave of emotional turmoil and self-punishment, and hold you back from thriving. It demands a personal (mostly unwarranted) admission of wrongdoing, of being unworthy or not quite enough. It may arise on occasions when someone feels—however inaccurately—that they haven't done as much as they could have, when they've not lived up to their own standards or have overstepped an invisible mark. A sense of guilt can even follow the acceptance of emotional or practical support. How often do people say sorry when they collapse in tears or ask a friend for help?

Guilt vs. Shame

Occasionally, guilt is projected onto a loved one—"don't make me feel guilty"—and can be triggered by self-proclaimed misdemeanors such as taking 20 minutes for an afternoon stroll in the park, eating so-called prohibited foods, or not spending enough time with family members. Then there's feeling guilty about . . . feeling guilty. Guilt's coconspirator is shame, and the terms are sometimes used interchangeably depending on the experience. Opening the Oxford English Dictionary once more, the noun "shame" is defined as "a painful feeling of humiliation or distress caused by the consciousness of wrong or foolish behavior" and "a loss of respect or esteem; dishonor." In practice, guilt is really how you feel about yourself, whereas shame is more closely associated with external actions or how you may have treated another person.

Judge and Jury

In this way, guilt is an act of self-sabotage causing self-suffering. Like carbon monoxide, it is silent, undetectable to others, and yet slowly affects physical and mental health. Guilt colonizes thoughts, dictates your self-narrative, and replays and reinforces negative patterns in the mind. It is to try yourself in your own court of law, find yourself culpable, and mete out self-punishment. Under examination, feelings of guilt seem rooted to anywhere or in anything other than the present moment—to the past or future, to what you feel you should be doing or what you should have done. "All forms of guilt, regret, resentment, sadness, and all forms of non-forgiveness are caused by too much past and not enough presence," says psychologist Eckhart Tolle.

Looking At the Self

Guilt and shame may be coconspirators, but their neighbors are self-esteem and self-worth. "Shame, guilt, embarrassment, and pride are members of a family of 'self-conscious emotions' evoked by self-reflection and self-evaluation," state psychologists June Price Tangney, Jeff Stuewig, and Debra J. Mashek in their 2007 paper "Moral Emotions and Moral Behaviour." They explain, "This self-evaluation may be implicit or explicit, consciously experienced or transpiring beneath the radar of our awareness. But importantly, the self is the object of these self-conscious emotions."

From Self-Guilt to Self-Compassion

With anything that is centered on the self, however, there is room for a positive dimension. The individual holds the power to change the situation. There is a beautiful prayer by Reinhold Niebuhr, a twentieth-century theologian, who explores this power of the present moment beautifully, "Grant me the serenity to accept the things I cannot change, the courage to change the things I can, and the wisdom to know the difference."

It's easy to forget you have the power to choose change. The practice of mindfulness and bringing conscious awareness to the present moment without judgment can encourage self-compassion while simultaneously turning down feelings of guilt. Self-sabotage can be turned into self-love.

How Can You Practice This?

In practical terms, this self-sabotage may look like a relaxed Saturday evening on the couch feeling guilty for not having cleaned up after dinner. Instead of relaxing, focusing on a book, TV show, or conversation, those minutes, hours, or the whole evening are spent in a state of unease because of what hasn't been done. This can spiral into feeling guilty about all manner of self-assigned chores that haven't been started let alone finished.

By bringing awareness to the present moment and acknowledging the momentary intoxication of guilt, you can remind yourself you have a choice. In this example, it is to leave your novel, show, or friend and finish the clearing-up or to stay where you are and enjoy the moment without guilt. It is an opportunity for action, self-compassion, and understanding. Rather than viewing feelings of guilt as another reason for self-punishment, take loving responsibility for it, reframe your self-judgment, and see it as a reminder for self-compassion.

EASE THE GUILT

The effectiveness of any self-care, meditation, or mindfulness practice requires just that—practice. And an element of self-awareness, cultivated through self-reflection, is then required through pausing, reflecting, reframing, and taking action.

1. Pause

It is helpful to get into the habit of pausing and asking: "How am I feeling?" This mindfulness practice can help to develop self-awareness and, by acknowledging certain feelings, it is possible to erode their power. It also offers the opportunity to choose a loving action for oneself and others. All self-perpetuated change begins with awareness.

- With eyes closed, take a deep breath.

- On the inhalation, notice the sensation of your breath entering your nostrils and the sensation of the air traveling down your throat.

- Notice your lungs and chest expand and your shoulders raise slightly.

- Effortlessly sigh the breath out and allow the weight of your body to drop down and relax.

- Repeat three times.

2. Reflect

With eyes open or closed, reflect for a moment on how you are feeling. Become curious about your emotions and try not to judge yourself for it. What you are experiencing right now, good or bad, is not you, it's just a feeling. It is human to go through all the emotions under the sun at some point in life, so relax and allow yourself to acknowledge the feeling. See this moment as a way to get to know yourself a little better and become clear on your own boundaries, values, or standards for yourself and others.

Voice your thoughts and write them down here.

....

....

....

....

....

....

....

....

....

....

....

....

....

....

....

3. Reframe

If your mind sends you a misleading message about guilt, recognize it as incorrect and label it as a false alarm. Ignore it as best you can and make a fresh effort to have a positive attitude.

Record any of these messages here, then explain why it's a false alarm below.

....

....

....

....

....

....

....

....

....

....

....

....

....

....

....

....

....

4. Act

Ask yourself what is the most loving action in that moment, "What would my best self do?" Taking action might not require any physical effort. It might mean allowing yourself guilt-free rest and relaxation or giving yourself permission to attend a yoga class you know you'll love once you get there. Remind yourself how you'll feel afterward as extra motivation to take positive steps.

It can be helpful to remember that guilt is an emotional response to negative thought patterns, often about oneself. By regularly practicing and prioritizing self-care, self-compassion, and mindfulness, you might notice a difference when it comes to your relationship with guilt. What will you do to silence the false alarm?

Write down some ideas and refer back to them when you need to.

....

....

....

....

....

....

....

....

....

....

....

....

....

....

Altered Ego

Remember pretending to be a superhero as a kid and feeling as though you could do anything? It turns out there's something in that childlike role-play that could be key to thriving as an adult.

People are often naturally suited to different roles in life, but that doesn't mean always having to stay in that role. If you feel you're missing a personality trait that you need to get ahead, for example, you can just go and find it—all you have to do is create an alter ego (which means "other self" in Latin). By molding a second version of yourself you can conquer an area of your life that your current version isn't obviously suited to. But this is the kind of thing usually reserved for the likes of rock stars and athletes, right? Not according to mindset expert Todd Herman, who, for the past twenty years, has been advising elite sports stars and business people on psychological methods to reach peak performance.

Achieve Your Goals

According to Todd, anyone can harness the power of an alternative personality to fit a goal they want to achieve. "Some people might think they aren't able to be more creative; others perhaps believe they can't stand up in front of others and speak dynamically. Whatever it is that people think they lack, an alter ego helps us to bypass that critical-thinking factor," he says. Todd believes the beauty of an alter ego is that it can also allow us to overcome any negative dialogue we're used to telling ourselves about why we can't do something, as "we're using our creative imagination to gracefully and elegantly sidestep that negative self-talk because now we're associating ourselves with a new identity."

Who Do You Want to Be?

It might seem slightly out of the ordinary, but multiple personalities are employed throughout life. If you think about it, people often present different versions of themselves to the world. For example, your work personality wouldn't necessarily be at home tucking your children into bed at night, the same way your parent personality might not be in a meeting with colleagues. Different traits suit different scenarios and will take us in various directions. "The dangerous thing is to think you've got just one identity," says Todd. "No, we don't. We've got many roles that we play, so the power of the alter ego is being very intentional about what role it is we're trying to be better at."

But we can't just switch on desirable personality traits we've never had before—can we? Many of us frequently sell ourselves a certain narrative that prevents us from doing something that feels unnatural. "Human beings act through whatever they associate themselves with," says Todd. "Somehow, someway, we don't see ourselves having the traits we want, so instead of acting as 'ourselves' we're using our creative imagination to release the traits we're associating with someone and something else."

"All the world's a stage, and all the men and women merely players; they have their exits and their entrances, and one man in his time plays many parts, his acts being seven ages."

William Shakespeare

Power of Props

It's been suggested through studies that we can change our personalities based on perception. A 2012 experiment at Northwestern University in Illinois showed just that. A group of undergraduates were given a white coat to wear during an attention and accuracy test. They were split into three groups—the first group wore what they were told was a doctor's coat, the second a painter's coat, and the third a lab coat. The group wearing the doctor's coat had the greatest level of attention, the group wearing the painter's coat behaved the most artistically, and the group wearing the lab coat was more cautious. All three groups were actually wearing the same white coat, but the students took on the traits of the profession that they were told the coat represented. This is proof that props, such as items of clothing, can signal the brain to act in a certain way.

Wear It Well

Civil rights activist Martin Luther King, Jr. wore a pair of glasses to help him feel more distinguished when he was giving speeches. In a similar way, Todd explains how British prime minister Winston Churchill used to stand in front of a wall of hats when he was feeling discouraged and ask himself, "Which self should I be today?" Props can help signal an alter ego, which "taps into the psychological phenomenon of enclothed cognition." He says it's the term used to describe how "human beings will adopt the traits of whatever they're wearing and exhibit them naturally." For example, if you don a white lab coat, you're going to become "more detailed, careful, and methodical because that's what we associate with the people who wear them."

FINDING YOUR ALTER EGO

Eventually, the different traits that you adopt could become part of your natural personality. "The face that you present to others," says Todd, "becomes the person that they believe you are. And when you find a way to identify with the strongest, most powerful version of yourself, that's the person you start growing into." Here's how to find your alter ego.

1. Establish Why You Need One
"Human beings always act in context," says Todd. Start by outlining what it is that you want to achieve.

Are you trying to conquer speaking on stage, do you want to get fitter, or are you trying to become a better parent?

....

....

....

....

....

....

2. Choose Your Personality Traits
Once you've decided on what you're trying to achieve, think about what kind of characteristics would help you. Todd advises asking yourself, "What traits do I want to show up with?"

How does your alter ego think? What are its defining attributes?

....

....

....

....

....

3. Visualize

It might feel like a tall order to conjure up a brand-new person in your head, so try thinking about people who you admire. Find someone who makes you think: "I wish I was more like that." Todd says, "It's a great starting place because in some way you are connected to that person. It could be Katniss Everdeen, it could be Daenerys Targaryen."

Write down some inspiring people whose traits you'd like your alter ego to have.

➤ ....

....

➤ ....

....

➤ ....

....

4. Find Your Object

Put enclothed cognition to the test. Find an object that will take you into the headspace of your alter ego. Todd's prop is a pair of glasses, but you could use anything from jewelry to an item of clothing.

What objects will your alter ego be wearing?

➤ ....

....

➤ ....

....

➤ ....

....

Nurturing Fresh Growth

Mistakes are part of life. Sometimes they're minor and have minimal effect, but occasionally they're more significant and cause hurt and distress. How do you move on, especially if others insist on reminding you about an event for which you're truly sorry?

Few people are without embarrassing moments or chapters in their lives, whether it's behavior they regret, words they'd love to take back, or actions they wish they had (or hadn't) taken. They're the events that bring no pride, but for which a genuine apology has been given and from which lessons have been learned. The injured party is not necessarily going to forget them or pretend they didn't happen, but it's time to try again. For some, however, the past is ever-present and they can't help but refer to previous misdemeanors time and time again.

Rehashing the Past
Whether it's a friend, partner, colleague, or family member, and whatever the nature of the current discussion or argument, some people struggle to stop themselves referring to mistakes you've made in the past, despite the fact that months (if not years) have passed and you've proved it was a one-off incident. It might not be intentional, or it could be that, for them, the issue wasn't resolved satisfactorily, so they'll keep bringing up that deadline you missed six months previously, the thirtieth birthday speech you bungled five years ago, or the vase you broke one Christmas.

What's the Motive?

If it's someone you don't know well or trust, they could be bringing up past mistakes in an effort to manipulate or shake your confidence. For example, a colleague continually referring to a missed deadline might perceive you as a threat to their progress and be using the incident to undermine your credibility. Another reason might be that they feel you haven't heard them or you've failed to understand their feelings. They want to ensure their upset is noted.

If it's a close friend or family member, they might not be doing it to hurt you (even if it feels that way). It could be that they're teasing you, or they might even believe that their constant reminders of a past error will ensure you don't repeat it and invite further negative experiences into your life.

Diversion Tactics

Often, however, it's a default strategy when a person is under pressure, especially if they themselves have made a mistake. If you're having a discussion with someone who feels that they're on the back foot, a quick comment about a previous misdemeanor committed by you takes the pressure off them and switches the focus. It works in the moment—a colleague might not have to listen to feedback about how they could improve their performance, for instance—but it also risks turning what might be a constructive conversation into a full-blown row, as you're forced once more to explain and apologize for the past. And, longer term, it's likely to cause growing resentment and annoyance, possibly at the eventual cost of a mutually constructive and respectful working relationship.

RESOLVING THE SITUATION

Learning how to move on from past regrets is possible.

1. Be at Peace with Your Past

If you get upset and defensive when others bring up past errors, it might mean you still feel bad about the incident. What happened, happened—you can't change that. Learn from it and forgive yourself. No one's perfect and everyone makes mistakes. If you've apologized and made amends, try not to allow others to make you feel bad about what you did or didn't do. It could be you've changed so much that you barely recognize the you who erred. Either way, you can view the past as your history and choose to focus on who you are now.

Think about a mistake you made in the past. What was it?

....
....
....
....

What lessons did it teach you?

....
....
....

How has the experience made you a better person today?

....
....
....
....

2. Understand the Other Person

Once you have control over your emotions, try to view the occasions when mistakes are recalled with a fresh perspective and work out why the other person is doing it—or whether they even realize they're dredging up the past in a way that might hurt you or cause distress or defensiveness. It might also be an indication that, for them, an issue hasn't been resolved despite the apologies you've already given. Where possible, try to state that you understand their position and reassure them you want to deal with it. It's easy and understandable to become defensive, but that kind of reaction is less likely to have a positive outcome, one where each party validates the other's feelings and agrees to work on creating a more positive relationship.

Think about a time when someone dredged up an old mistake in a way that hurt you. When was it? What was the mistake?

....

....

....

....

Now reflect on why they might have felt the need to do it. What was it about that particular situation? Maybe there are clues in the other person's behavior that indicates their mindset at the time. Jot down your thoughts here. It might help you to write from their perspective and in their voice.

....

....

....

....

....

....

....

3. Talk to Them

You could start by telling your colleague, partner, or relative how it makes you feel when they continually bring up your mistakes. Calmly explain that while you understand it caused them problems or distress, you're hurt that it's still being mentioned. It might help to emphasize how much you care for and value them and that you acknowledge and take responsibility for how your actions affected them. It's equally important, however, to reiterate that you've apologized, made amends, and learned from the mistake, and that while you can't change the past, you're more than willing to resolve any current problems.

If it feels like there's still tension or distress about what happened, you could suggest talking it through, in an effort to understand and finally resolve the situation. It might be that their trust in you or the relationship has been dented. If this is the case, ask how you can work together to rebuild it. It might take hard work and a renewed effort from both parties, but it's possible that, in time, you can both look forward without negating the past.

Write down what you might say now in response to your past error being brought up.

....

....

....

....

....

....

....

....

....

....

....

4. When You're Holding a Grudge

If you're reading this and realize you're the one bringing up the past, remember you have the power to forgive and accept if not forgive and forget. Whether it's a missed deadline, a bungled birthday speech, a broken vase, or a betrayal of trust, explore how you feel about the incident and think about how you might want to move forward with the person who upset or let you down.

If you haven't forgiven them or feel the issue is unresolved, try to find a way to open up to them about it. It might help to talk to a close friend first or write it down on paper so that you can more fully articulate your feelings. In this way it's less likely to subconsciously erode your relationship. If they genuinely apologize and validate your feelings and you still value and want them in your life, it might be it's time to accept what happened and try not to allow it to affect your future.

Use this space to explore an unresolved incident fully. What feelings do you have? Why do you think you aren't over the issue yet?

....

....

....

....

....

How is this incident holding back your relationship with the other person? What would you like to express to them?

....

....

....

....

....

....

A Sense of Pride

Do you fear that telling others about your accomplishments will make you seem big-headed or boastful? Why? You deserve to feel good about what you've achieved, and you're worthy of praise.

Why is it that some people are deeply reluctant to proudly share news of their achievements? Maybe it's a cultural thing, or maybe it's personal and varies from human to human. Perhaps there's that fear of being seen as full of hot air but with little to show for it. Or maybe it's the worry of being seen as overloaded with self-importance and that this will equate to being unlikable or unpopular.

Can there be any positive aspects in talking up achievements and flagging praiseworthy accomplishments, even if that might prompt negative comments from others? And what exactly is the difference between a robust sense of self-worth and a fragile ego, puffed up with pride and in need of constant reassurance?

Authentic vs. Hubristic

Greek philosopher Aristotle described pride as the "crown of the virtues." He argues that well-deserved praise, from good people for good deeds and accomplishments, is a virtue. It's important to see here what Aristotle is driving at: the person who is justly proud believes themselves to be worthy of praise because they are worthy of praise.

For the rest, who are not so worthy, this pride is, in fact, just vanity. Whether you agree with this take on *Cogito, ergo sum* ("I think, therefore I am") or not, it does spell out one thing—being proud, or not, is in the eye of the beholder. One person's rightful recognition of achievement is another's inflated sense of self-importance. Guy Winch, a psychologist and author, says, "Psychologists distinguish between two kinds of pride. Authentic pride arises when we feel good about ourselves, confident and productive, and is related to socially desirable personality traits such as being agreeable, conscientious, and emotionally stable. Hubristic pride tends to involve egotism and arrogance, and is related to socially undesirable traits such as being disagreeable, aggressive, having low or brittle self-esteem—and being prone to shame."

From this, it's clear that, for psychologists and philosophers at least, pride is not always a negative emotion or character trait. It has a key role to play in a person's feelings of self-worth, if deemed to be authentic. It's a complicated emotion to untangle, but it does seem to be different from a high sense of self-worth.

Recognizing What Matters

Writer, therapist, and lecturer John Amodeo describes the difficulty in clinging on to the material things that make you proud, such as a new car or a promotion—things that ultimately lose their worth and do not provide long-term happiness. Instead, he says, "A more genuine and stable self-worth is based upon validating, affirming, and valuing ourselves as we are. Self-worth is a function of living with dignity, which exists apart from any accomplishments. Achievements are ephemeral and can become a trap. If too much of our attention goes toward accomplishing bigger and better things in order to feel good, then we become addicted to external sources of gratification."

He suggests that for pride to be replaced with a healthy sense of self-worth, you could draw a sense of achievement from the elements of life that aren't fleeting. Focus on relationships, the care you take over your work, and any other elements that could be defined as more spiritual in nature. This, in turn, leads to a more stable, more sustainable way of feeling and provides a foundation for healthy self-esteem that doesn't rely on things or objects, or comparing yourself to others.

Once you are aware of the ups and downs of pride and the necessity of a healthy sense of self-worth, how then do you react when you want to shout about your accomplishments? Maybe, for once, you should do just that (figuratively speaking). Use social media channels, the office, or friendship groups to let everyone know exactly how proud you are of that achievement, be it completing a marathon, bagging a well-deserved promotion, or passing an exam at night school. Perhaps you'll employ the so-called "humble brag," dressing up a boast in language that appears laced in humility.

Good Intentions

Surely, it can't do any harm to seek some adulation and congratulations from others once in a while? The answer is, of course, it doesn't. Taking pride in your achievements, more so than your things, is nothing to be ashamed of, especially if they're the result of hard work and dedication. If your expression comes from a genuine sense of accomplishment, then you know your announcement is given with the best intention and you should receive the affirmation of others without fear of sounding boastful.

Success is nothing to be ashamed of and can be the driving force needed to spur on others toward creating successes of their own. The issue may come down to a question of nuance. When talking about your latest achievement at work, who are you talking to? That acquaintance who's struggling with a boss who doesn't recognize or value them? Or the friend who's just been made redundant and is scared for the future? Audience plays a key role in how you're received.

Exploring the concepts of pride and valuing your self-worth are crucial pieces to the jigsaw puzzle that is your personality. If you worry that you're beginning to sound puffed up, overly proud, and arrogant, as therapist Guy says, this very fear alone will mean that's something you'll never become.

The key, as with most complicated elements of life, is to find balance and stay tuned into your relationships with friends, family, and colleagues. Hubristic pride has little place in the development of healthy relationships and is a world away from authentic pride and great self-esteem. Focus on the characteristics of these two traits to keep friendships and relationships free from strain and live a happier, more balanced life by focusing on what's important.

BALANCING ACT

Consider this advice before shouting about your success:

- Don't be afraid to talk about how and why you got there, but consider your audience and what it is you're talking about.

- Think carefully before telling your friend on a lower income about your latest purchase. Consider if anyone really needs to know about how proud you are of your latest luxury item.

- But when you've truly achieved something, talk about it—tell those who love you how thrilled you are to have finally got to where you need to be after so long striving for it. You deserve it!

TIME TO SHARE?

If you're not sure whether to relay your accomplishments to the wider world, then try these exercises, which might help you to make a more informed decision.

1. Fact or Fiction?
Record the facts of your achievement. Don't exaggerate. Just describe what happened.

....

....

....

....

....

....

Now write down the response you would like your friend/family member to give.

....

....

....

....

....

....

....

Note down the probable response you think they'll give.

....

....

....

....

....

....

....

If there are significant differences between your last two answers, write down the reasons why you think this might be. Take time to think about your answers and make a decision that feels appropriate.

....

....

....

....

....

....

....

....

....

2. Question Your Motivations

Are you looking for affirmation from a particular person? Are you hoping to impress or shame them, or do you simply want to share the latest news in your life? Be honest with yourself.

....

....

....

....

....

....

....

....

....

....

....

....

....

....

....

If you find a less-than-positive reason or you know they're going through a tough time, hold off.

3. Positive Pride

Telling others about your accomplishments can boost your confidence, inspire others, and reveal who you really are.

Can you look back at a recent accomplishment and extract the lessons you learned along the way?

....

....

....

....

....

....

How might you offer those lessons to support, inspire, and encourage others?

....

....

....

....

....

....

....

....

....

....

STERLING
New York

An Imprint of Sterling Publishing Co., Inc.

STERLING and the distinctive Sterling logo are registered trademarks of
Sterling Publishing Co., Inc.

© 2021 The Guild of Master Craftsmen Publications Ltd.

ISBN 978-1-4549-4400-3

Distributed in Canada by Sterling Publishing Co., Inc.
c/o Canadian Manda Group, 664 Annette Street
Toronto, Ontario M6S 2C8, Canada

For information about custom editions, special sales, and premium and corporate
purchases, please contact Sterling Special Sales at 800-805-5489 or
specialsales@sterlingpublishing.com.

Manufactured in Singapore

2 4 6 8 10 9 7 5 3 1

sterlingpublishing.com

Editorial: Susie Duff, Samita Foria, Catherine Kielthy, Jane Roe
Design: Jo Chapman
Publisher: Jonathan Grogan

Words credits: Dawattie Basdeo, Jessica Chivers, Gabriela Cordero, Ruby Deevoy,
Kerry Dolan, Laura Gabrielle Feasey, Donna Findlay, Katie Holloway, Joanna Hulin,
Kate Orson, Caroline Pattenden, Dean Ratore, Sarah Rodrigues, Amy Schofield,
Simone Scott, Carol Anne Strange, Gabrielle Treanor

Illustrations: Holly Acland, Agnese Bicocchi, Louise Billyard, Rialda Dizdarevic,
Chiara Lanzieri, Amy Leonard, Carla Llanos, Irina Perju, Sophie Standing,
Silvia Stecher, Kate Styling, Sirin Thada, Sara Thielker, Michelle Urra,
Kimberley Laura Walker, Ellice Weaver
Cover illustration: Carla Llanos